THE GRAPHIC NOVEL
William Shakespeare

QUICK TEXT VERSION

Script Adaptation: John McDonald
Character Designs & Original Artwork: Jon Haward
Inking: Gary Erskine
Colouring & Lettering: Nigel Dobbyn
Design & Layout: Jo Wheeler & Carl Andrews

Editor in Chief: Clive Bryant

The Tempest: The Graphic Novel
Quick Text Version

William Shakespeare

First UK Edition

Published by: Classical Comics Ltd

Acknowledgments: Every effort has been made to trace copyright holders of
material reproduced in this book. Any rights not acknowledged here will be
acknowledged in subsequent editions if notice is given to Classical Comics Ltd.

Images on page 135 reproduced with the kind permission of The Shakespeare Birthplace Trust.

All enquiries should be addressed to:
Classical Comics Ltd.
PO Box 7280
Litchborough
Towcester
NN12 9AR
United Kingdom
Tel: 0845 812 3000

info@classicalcomics.com
www.classicalcomics.com

ISBN: 978-1-906332-31-0

Printed in the UK

This book is printed by The Charlesworth Group using biodegradable vegetable inks,
on environmentally friendly paper which is FSC
certified (TT-COC-002868). This material can be disposed of by recycling,
incineration for energy recovery, composting and biodegradation.

Mixed Sources
Product group from well-managed
forests and other controlled sources
www.fsc.org Cert no. TT-COC-002868
© 1996 Forest Stewardship Council
FSC

The publisher wishes to acknowledge and thank Joe Sutliff Sanders and Greg Powell
for their help in the completion of this book.

The rights of John McDonald, Jon Haward, Gary Erskine and Nigel Dobbyn
to be identified as the artists of this work have been asserted in accordance with
the Copyright, Designs and Patents Act 1988 sections 77 and 78.

Contents

Dramatis Personæ

Prospero
The right Duke of Milan

Miranda
Prospero's daughter

Caliban
A savage and deformed slave

Ariel
An airy Spirit

Alonso
King of Naples

Ferdinand
The King's son

Sebastian
The King's brother

Antonio
Prospero's brother, the usurping Duke of Milan

Gonzalo
An honest old counsellor

Adrian
A lord

Francisco
A lord

Stephano
A drunken butler

Trinculo
A jester

Master of the ship

Boatswain of the ship
(pronounced "Bo'sun")

Mariners of the ship

Ceres, Juno and Iris
Spirits, commanded by Prospero

Spirits and Reapers
Commanded by Prospero

Prologue

A royal ship, carrying the King of Naples and his
entourage, is part of a small fleet sailing home
from Tunis in North Africa. They are returning
from the wedding of the King's daughter, Claribel,
to the King of Tunis. The King of Naples is
accompanied by his son Ferdinand, his brother
Sebastian, and his trusty advisor Gonzalo. Also
with the party is the King's friend Antonio, Duke
of Milan. Antonio took the title of Duke from his
older brother Prospero, who disappeared suddenly
one night, never to be seen again…

Milan

Corsica

Sardinia

Naples

Sicily

Algiers

Tunis

MEDITERI

The Tempest

Cyprus

Paphos

Crete

NEAN SEA

N
W E
S

IT WAS *TWELVE YEARS AGO.* YOUR *FATHER* WAS *DUKE OF MILAN* --

BUT, *YOU'RE* MY FATHER --

-- *I* WAS *DUKE OF MILAN,* AND *YOU* WERE MY *PRINCESS.*

HOW DID WE END UP *HERE?*

WAS IT A *CRIME* AGAINST US, OR WERE WE *LUCKY?*

BOTH, MY DEAR GIRL!

IT WAS A *CRIME* THAT WE WERE *DRIVEN AWAY,* BUT WE WERE *LUCKY* TO END UP *HERE.*

IT MUST BE VERY *PAINFUL* FOR YOU TO *REMEMBER* THIS, FATHER.

MY BROTHER, ANTONIO –

ARE YOU *LISTENING?*

MY BROTHER, ANTONIO, WAS *DISLOYAL* TO ME.

17

DO YOU *HEAR?*

YOUR *STORY* WOULD CURE *DEAFNESS.*

SO HE HAD TO *BECOME* THE *DUKE* OF *MILAN.*

HE BELIEVED THAT *I* WAS *NO* LONGER CAPABLE OF *RULING.*

HE FOUND A *FRIEND* IN THE *KING* OF *NAPLES,* AND *ANTONIO* PROMISED TO PAY HIM *MONEY* IF HE BECAME *DUKE.*

GOODNESS ME!

SHOULD HE BE CALLED MY *BROTHER* AFTER THAT?

SOME *GOOD MOTHERS* HAVE BAD SONS.

THE *KING OF NAPLES* WAS MY *ENEMY.*

HE AGREED TO HELP MY BROTHER *GET RID* OF ME.

AN *ARMY* WAS GATHERED, AND THEY DRAGGED US AWAY IN THE *MIDDLE OF THE NIGHT.* I STILL REMEMBER HOW YOU *CRIED.*

waaah -awah

I MUST HAVE BEEN A *WORRY* FOR YOU.

NO – YOU *KEPT ME GOING.* YOUR *SMILE* HELPED ME THROUGH THAT *TERRIBLE TIME.*

HOW DID WE *GET* HERE?

MY *FRIEND* GONZALO HAD PUT SOME *FOOD AND WATER* IN THE BOAT, ALONG WITH *CLOTHES AND BLANKETS.*

HE ALSO PUT IN MANY *BOOKS* FROM MY *LIBRARY.*

I HOPE I CAN *MEET* HIM SOMEDAY.

WE LANDED ON THIS *ISLAND,* AND I HAVE BEEN YOUR *TEACHER* EVER SINCE.

I STILL DON'T UNDERSTAND WHY YOU MADE THE *STORM.*

BY LUCK, MY *ENEMIES* HAVE BEEN *BROUGHT TO OUR ISLAND.*

I FEEL THAT I MUST *TAKE THIS CHANCE* – BUT *NO MORE QUESTIONS* FOR NOW.

EVERYONE EXCEPT THE SAILORS *JUMPED* INTO THE SEA TO GET AWAY FROM THE *BURNING* SHIP.

THE KING'S SON, FERDINAND, JUMPED *FIRST*, SHOUTING THAT *"THE DEVILS ARE HERE!"*

WELL DONE, MY SPIRIT.

ARE THEY ALL *SAFE*, ARIEL?

NO ONE WAS HURT.

EVEN THEIR *CLOTHES* ARE DRY AND FRESH. I'VE *SCATTERED* THEM IN *GROUPS* AROUND THE ISLAND AS YOU ORDERED.

THE KING'S SON IS ALONE.

55

71

81

84

KA-RAKK!

YOU MUST BE *PUNISHED* FOR THAT TERRIBLE CRIME.

ALONSO, YOU HAVE *LOST YOUR SON.*

THE ONLY WAY YOU CAN ESCAPE A *SLOW DEATH* HERE ON THIS ISLAND IS TO BE SINCERELY SORRY FOR WHAT YOU HAVE DONE, AND PROMISE TO LIVE *GOOD LIVES* FROM NOW ON.

BUT THE TIME HAS COME TO *STOP* – I MUST CONJURE UP *ONE FINAL SPELL.*

ARIEL, GET ME THE **CLOTHES** I WORE WHEN I WAS **DUKE OF MILAN**.

YOU'LL BE FREE **VERY SOON**.

HAPPILY, HAPPILY, I WILL LIVE **FREE**, UNDER THE **FLOWERS** THAT HANG FROM THE **TREE**.

I'LL **MISS** YOU, ARIEL, BUT I'LL **STILL** SET YOU **FREE** VERY SOON.

GO TO THE **KING'S SHIP** AND BRING THE **MASTER** AND THE **BOATSWAIN** HERE.

I'LL BE **BACK** BEFORE YOU **KNOW** IT.

115

117

120

123

THIS IS THE *STRANGEST THING* I HAVE EVER *KNOWN.* WE NEED SOMEONE TO *EXPLAIN* IT ALL.

DON'T TROUBLE YOUR MIND WITH THAT FOR *NOW* --

-- I SHALL EXPLAIN EVERYTHING *LATER.*

ARIEL, SET *CALIBAN* AND HIS FRIENDS *FREE.*

A COUPLE OF YOUR *MEN* ARE STILL *MISSING.*

127

The Tempest

End

William Shakespeare

(c.1564 - 1616 AD)

National Portrait Gallery, London

Shakespeare is, without question, the world's most famous playwright. Yet, despite his fame, very few records and artefacts exist for him — we don't even know the exact date of his birth! April 23rd 1564 (St George's Day) is taken to be his birthday, as this was three days before his baptism (for which we do have a record). Records also tell us that he died on the same date in 1616, aged fifty-two.

The life of William Shakespeare can be divided into three acts.

Act One – Stratford-upon-Avon

William was the eldest son of tradesman John Shakespeare and Mary Arden, and the third of eight children (he had two older sisters). The Shakespeares were a respectable family. The year after William was born, John (who made gloves and traded leather) became an alderman of Stratford-upon-Avon, and four years later he became High Bailiff (or mayor) of the town.

Little is known of William's childhood. He learnt to read and write at the local primary school, and later is believed to have attended the local grammar school, where he studied Latin and English Literature. In 1582, aged eighteen, William married a local farmer's daughter, Anne Hathaway. Anne was eight years his senior and three months pregnant. During their marriage they had three children: Susanna, born on 26th May 1583 and twins, Hamnet and Judith, born on 2nd February 1585. Hamnet (William's only son) died in 1596, aged eleven, from Bubonic Plague.

Act Two – London

Five years into his marriage, in 1587, William's wife and children stayed in Stratford, while he moved to London. He appeared as an actor at *The Theatre* (England's first permanent theatre) and gave public recitals of his own poems; but it was his playwriting that created the most interest. His fame soon spread far and wide. When Queen Elizabeth I died in 1603, the new King James I (who was already King James VI of Scotland) gave royal consent for Shakespeare's acting company, *The Lord Chamberlain's Men* to be called *The King's Men* in return for entertaining the court. This association was to shape a number of plays, such as *Macbeth*, which was written to please the Scottish King.

William Shakespeare is attributed with writing and collaborating on 38 plays, 154 sonnets and 5 poems, in just twenty-three years between 1590 and 1613. No original manuscript exists for any of his plays, making it hard to accurately date any of them. Printing was still in its infancy, and plays tended to change as they were performed. Shakespeare would write manuscript for the actors and continue to refine them over a number of performances. The plays we know today have survived from written copies taken at various stages of each play and usually written by the actors from memory. This has given rise to variations in texts of what is now known as "quarto" versions of the plays, until we reach the first official printing of each play in the 1623 "folio" *Mr William Shakespeare's Comedies, Histories, & Tragedies*. His last solo-authored work was *The Tempest* in 1611, which was only followed by collaborative work on two plays (*Henry VIII* and *Two Noble Kinsmen*) with John Fletcher. Shakespeare is strongly associated with the famous *Globe Theatre*. Built by his troupe in 1599, it became his "spiritual home", with thousands of people crammed into the small space for each performance. There were 3,000 people in the building in 1613 when a cannon-shot during a performance of *Henry VIII* set fire to the thatched roof and the entire theatre was burnt to the ground. Although it was rebuilt a year later, it marked an end to Shakespeare's writing and to his time in London.

Act Three - Retirement

Shortly after the 1613 accident at *The Globe*, Shakespeare left the capital and returned to live once more with his family in Stratford-upon-Avon. He died on April 23rd 1616 and was buried two days later at the Church of the Holy Trinity (the same church where he had been baptised fifty-two years earlier). The cause of his death remains unknown.

Epilogue

At the time of his death, Shakespeare had substantial properties, which he bestowed on his family and associates from the theatre. He had no son to inherit his wealth, and he left the majority of his possessions to his eldest daughter Susanna. Curiously, the only thing that he left to his wife Anne was his second-best bed! (although she continued to live in the family home after his death). William Shakespeare's last direct descendant died in 1670. She was his granddaughter, Elizabeth.

Shakespeare Birthplace Trust

As so few relics survive from Shakespeare's life, it is amazing that the house where he was born and raised remains intact. It is owned and cared for by the Shakespeare Birthplace Trust, which looks after a number of houses in the area:

Shakespeare's Birthplace

- Shakespeare's Birthplace.
- Mary Arden's Farm: The childhood home of Shakespeare's mother.
- Anne Hathaway's Cottage: The childhood home of Shakespeare's wife.
- Hall's Croft: The home of Shakespeare's eldest daughter, Susanna.
- New Place: Only the grounds exist of the house where Shakespeare died in 1616.
- Nash's House: The home of Shakespeare's granddaughter.

www.shakespeare.org.uk

Martin Droeshout's engraving of Shakespeare

Formed in 1847, the Trust also works to promote Shakespeare around the world. In early 2009, it announced that it had found a new Shakespeare portrait, believed to have been painted within his lifetime, with a trail of provenance that links it to Shakespeare himself.

It is accepted that Martin Droeshout's engraving (left) that appears on the First Folio of 1623 is an authentic likeness of Shakespeare because the people involved in its publication would have personally known him. This new portrait (once owned by Henry Wriothesley, 3rd Earl of Southampton, one of Shakespeare's most loyal supporters) is so similar in all facial aspects that it is now suspected to have been the source that Droeshout used for his famous engraving. **www.shakespearefound.org.uk**

History of The Tempest

The Tempest was almost certainly Shakespeare's last solo-authored work. Only *Henry VIII* and *Two Noble Kinsmen* were to follow, and they were both collaborations with John Fletcher. It is also the only Shakespeare play that features an original story — all of his other plays have very clear sources. Perhaps it is these two factors that prompt many to believe it to be his finest work — a view shared by the publishers of his first collected works (the "First Folio" of 1623), who gave pride of place to the play.

As with all of his plays, an accurate dating of *The Tempest* is near-impossible; however, we know that it was performed for King James I in November 1611, and this leads us to believe it was written earlier that same year (it was such a success that it was played again the following year to celebrate the betrothal of King James' daughter Elizabeth).

Shakespeare effectively retired after writing *The Tempest*, returning to Stratford-upon-Avon to live his final few years close to his family. Prospero's closing speech of the play appears to be a metaphor for Shakespeare "saying goodbye" to the profession and bowing out from the theatre altogether. The fact that he was soon to write his will and tidy up his business affairs means that this is unlikely to have been a coincidence.

Although it was performed in court, it wasn't written for any particular royal performance; however, it was almost certainly written with the King and his daughter in mind. Not only does it feature magic and witchcraft to pander to the King's interests, but it portrays an all-seeing and all-knowing father who protects and looks after the interests of his own daughter. The play also features a "masque" (the dance performed by the goddesses Iris, Ceres and Juno on pages 98-103). Masques were extremely popular in the royal courts and here also served as an interlude or resting point in the progress of the story.

The opening storm of thunder, coupled with shouting and peril, was a wonderfully effective way to grab the attention of the audience. Shakespeare uses the device brilliantly, as the storm also cuts the characters off from one another and separates reality from fantasy — not only for the players, but also for the on-lookers, as the actors land on the mysterious, magical island.

Sources

Exploration and colonisation of the "New World" were topical subjects in the early 1600s. Only 24 years before *The Tempest* was written, Sir Walter Raleigh had returned from his attempts to start colonies in North America. One such colony was established on Roanoke Island, off the coast of North Carolina, Virginia; but when supply ships revisited the colony four years later, all of the inhabitants had disappeared, and they became known as the "Lost Colony". Despite such stories, the expansion of British interests via colonisation continued, building up a romantic notion of valiant expeditions and the "taming" of the savage inhabitants of far-off lands.

Travellers brought back many strange tales, and some were documented, giving Shakespeare the inspiration for his masterpiece. The reports talked of cannibals and primitive people who conducted bizarre rituals. They were only vaguely human — much like Shakespeare's portrayal of Caliban (it is thought that the name of Caliban purposefully sounds similar to the word "cannibal"). Caliban's primitiveness, forced into civilisation by Prospero, reflects a positive view of colonisation that would have found favour with King James, justifying the many expeditions that the King funded. Shakespeare also cleverly portrays Caliban's resentment of Prospero's intrusion and enforced civilisation, which robbed Caliban of his ruling status on the island. This is quickly dismissed within the play. Not only does Shakespeare reveal Caliban's poor character in the recounting of his attack on Miranda (pages 36-37), but he clearly shows how Prospero was able to release the hidden power of the island, making it a better place for his arrival.

The inspiration for the storm itself came from a pamphlet printed in 1610 called *A Discovery of the Bermudas, other wise called the Ile of Divels*. It documented the story of how a convoy of ships, travelling from London to Virginia, encountered a storm that separated the flagship from the rest. The flagship was blown towards Bermuda and, although the ship was lost, no one drowned. The travellers lived on the island until they could build boats and sail on to Virginia. The story captured the minds of the exploration-hungry citizens of England and gave Shakespeare a dramatic starting point for his play.

Prospero
Prospero is shown to be a caring, brilliant and learned father with magical powers (which would have appealed to King James I). Like the King, his power is signified by his books, his staff and his robe. Books not only provided knowledge, but they were seen as a source of mystical power; particularly by the largely illiterate public. The figure of Prospero is thought to have been inspired by Queen Elizabeth's astrologer, Dr John Dee (1527-1608). Dee had a reputation for performing acts of magic and was renowned for possessing a vast library of books — at one time the

largest library in England. The mystical power that people believed he derived from his books was so feared that a group of people attacked his house and set fire to his library. King James I put an end to his financial support, and Dee was forced to sell his possessions. He died in poverty three years before *The Tempest* was written.

Theatre Development
From 1608, Shakespeare's acting troupe started to perform his plays at *Blackfriars Theatre* on the north bank of the River Thames in London. His "spiritual home", *The Globe Theatre*, was an open-air performance space and was subject to the effects of weather (the

"groundling" audience had no shelter from rain). *Blackfriars Theatre*, on the other hand, was a fully enclosed space that included lighting and a pipe organ. *The Tempest* was shaped by the availability of this facility. The play features the most music of any of his works, using the organ to full effect, as well as the backstage areas for sound effects and other "off-stage" music. Also, the "imaginary banquet" scene (pages 87-93) is stage-directed for the sudden appearance and disappearance of the table and the food. This was made possible by a trap door on the stage, with the area beneath open for the moving of props — something that *The Globe Theatre* didn't possess. This was theatre at the forefront of technology in 1611. It was important for Shakespeare to always be coming up with new spectacles, and one can only imagine how ending his fulltime writing career "on a high" with *The Tempest* would have left him satisfied in his final few remaining years.

Page Creation

Page 35 from the script of *The Tempest* showing the three text versions.

1. Script

The first stage in creating a graphic novel adaptation of a Shakespeare play is to split the original script into comic book panels, describing the images to be drawn as well as the dialogue, captions and sound effects. To do this, not only does the script writer need to know the play well, but he also needs to visualise each page in his head as he writes the art descriptions for each panel (there are over 460 panels in *The Tempest*).

Once this is created, the dialogue is adapted into Plain Text and Quick Text to create the three versions of the book, which all use the same artwork.

2. Character Sheets

As well as creating the script, the scriptwriter (John McDonald) also supplies descriptions of each character. The artist (Jon Haward) couples these with his own ideas to create a number of character sheets. These sheets provide a point of reference when drawing the pages, but more importantly they allow the artist to familiarise himself with the characters — to the point where they almost take on a life of their own.

A character sheet of Prospero and Ariel.

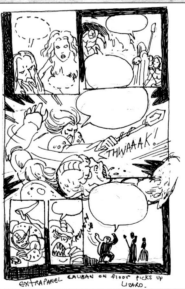

3. Rough Sketch

There is a wealth of detail in each panel of this book, and therefore it is important to solve any problems in the layouts through the use of rough sketches of each page. Here is Jon's sketch of page 35. Comparing it to the finished page, you can see how slight alterations were made during the artistic process.

Note how the characters were reversed in panel 2, to help with the lettering and also to have Prospero continuing in speaking from left to right, leading the reader on through the page.

The rough sketch created from the script.

4. Pencils

As soon as the rough sketch is approved by the editor, work starts on pencilling the page. The artwork is drawn on A3 art board at approximately 150% of the finished printed size. Here you can clearly see the change to panel 2, and the amount of detail that goes in to each and every panel, even at this early stage.

The pencil drawing of page 35.

5. Inks

The inking stage is important because it clarifies the pencil lines and finalises the linework. There is far more to this than simply tracing over the pencil lines! The best way to view inking is as a pre-colouring stage, where deep blacks are created, and certain textures added. Different line thicknesses are used to create a sense of depth in the image, and also to imply the types of edges being portrayed in the various materials.

The inked image, ready to be coloured.

6. Colouring

Adding colour really brings the page and its characters to life. Colouring isn't merely a process of replacing the white areas with flat colour. Some of the linework itself is shaded, while great emphasis is placed upon texture and light sources to get realistic shadows and highlights. Effects are also considered, such as the glow from Prospero's staff.. Finally, the whole page is colour-balanced to the other pages of that scene, and to the overall book.

The final coloured artwork.

The finished page 35 with Quick Text lettering.

7. Lettering

The final stage is to add the captions, sound effects, and speech bubbles from the script. These are placed on top of the finished coloured pages. Three versions of each page are lettered, one for each of the three versions of the book (Original Text, Plain Text and Quick Text).

Original Text

ISBN: 978-1-906332-29-7

Plain Text

ISBN: 978-1-906332-30-3

Quick Text

ISBN: 978-1-906332-31-0

Shakespeare's Globe

The Globe Theatre and Shakespeare

It is hard to appreciate today how theatres were actually a new idea in William Shakespeare's time. The very first theatre in Elizabethan London to only show plays, aptly called *The Theatre*, was introduced by an entrepreneur by the name of James Burbage. In fact, *The Globe Theatre*, possibly the most famous theatre of that era, was built from the timbers of *The Theatre*. The landlord of *The Theatre* was Giles Allen, a Puritan who disapproved of theatrical entertainment. When he decided to enforce a huge rent increase in the winter of 1598, the theatre members dismantled the building piece by piece and shipped it across the Thames to Southwark for reassembly. Allen was powerless to do anything, as the company owned the wood - although he spent three years in court trying to sue the perpetrators!

The report of the dismantling party (written by Schoenbaum) says: *"ryotous... armed... with divers and manye unlawfull and offensive weapons... in verye ryotous outragious and forcyble manner and contrarye to the lawes of your highnes Realme... and there pulling breaking and throwing downe the sayd Theater in verye outragious violent and riotous sort to the great disturbance and terrefyeing not onlye of your subjectes... but of divers others of your majesties loving subjectes there neere inhabitinge."*

William Shakespeare became a part owner of this new *Globe Theatre* in 1599. It was one of four major theatres in the area, along with the *Swan*, the *Rose*, and the *Hope*. The exact physical structure of the *Globe* is unknown, although scholars are fairly sure of some details through drawings from the period. The theatre itself was a closed structure with an open courtyard where the stage stood. Tiered galleries around the open area accommodated the wealthier patrons who could afford seats, and those of the lower classes - the "groundlings" - stood around the platform or "thrust" stage during the performance of a play. The space under and behind the stage was used for special effects, storage and costume changes. Surprisingly, although the entire structure was not very big by modern standards, it is known to have accommodated fairly large crowds - as many as 3,000 people - during a single performance.

The Globe II

In 1613, the original *Globe Theatre* burned to the ground when a cannon shot during a performance of *Henry VIII* set fire to the thatched roof of the gallery. Undeterred, the company completed a new *Globe* (this time with a tiled roof) on the foundations of its predecessor. Shakespeare didn't write any new plays for this theatre, which opened in 1614. He retired to Stratford-Upon-Avon that year, and died two years later. Despite that, performances continued until 1642, when the Puritans closed down all theatres and places of entertainment. Two years later, the Puritans razed the building to the ground in order to build tenements upon the site. No more was to be seen of the *Globe* for 352 years.

Shakespeare's Globe

Led by the vision of the late Sam Wanamaker, work began on the construction of a new *Globe* in 1993, close to the site of the original theatre. It was completed three years later, and Queen Elizabeth II officially opened the *New Globe Theatre* on June 12th, 1997 with a production of *Henry V*.

The *New Globe Theatre* is as faithful a reproduction as possible to the Elizabethan theatre, given that the details of the original are only known from sketches of the time. The building can accommodate 1,500 people in all, across the galleries and the "groundlings".

www.shakespeares-globe.org

Teaching Resource Packs

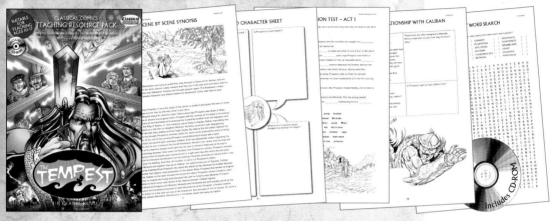

To accompany each title in our series of graphic novels and to help with their application in the classroom, we also publish teaching resource packs. These widely acclaimed 100+ page books are spiral-bound, making the pages easy to photocopy. They also include a CD-ROM with the pages in PDF format, ideal for whole-class teaching on whiteboards, laptops, etc or for direct digital printing. These books are written by teachers, for teachers, helping students to engage in the play or novel. Suitable for teaching ages 10-17, each book provides exercises that cover structure,

listening, understanding, motivation and character as well as key words, themes and literary techniques. Although the majority of the tasks focus on the use of language and comprehension, there are also many cross-curriculum topics, covering areas within history, ICT, drama, reading, speaking, writing and art. An extensive Educational Links section provides further study opportunities. Devised to encompass a broad range of skill levels, they provide many opportunities for differentiated teaching and the tailoring of lessons to meet individual needs.

"Thank you! These will be fantastic for all our students. It is a brilliant resource and to have the lesson ideas too are great. Thanks again to all your team who have created these."
B.P. KS3

"As to the resource, I can't wait to start using it! Well done on a fantastic service."
Will

"...you've certainly got a corner of East Anglia convinced that this is a fantastic way to teach and progress English literature and language!"
Chris

OUR RANGE OF TEACHING RESOURCE PACKS AVAILABLE

The Tempest
978-1-906332-40-2

Romeo & Juliet
978-1-906332-39-6

Macbeth
978-1-907127-01-4

Henry V
978-1-907127-00-7

Frankenstein
978-1-907127-03-8

Jane Eyre
978-1-907127-02-1

A Christmas Carol
978-1-907127-04-5

Great Expectations
978-1-906332-13-6

- Only £19.99 each

- 100+ spiral-bound, photocopiable pages.

- Electronic version included for whole-class teaching and digital printing.

- Cross-curricular topics and activities.

- Ideal for differentiated teaching.